First Library of Knowledge

Stars
and
Planets

BLACKBIRCH PRESS
An imprint of Thomson Gale, a part of The Thomson Corporation

Detroit • New York • San Francisco • San Diego • New Haven, Conn. • Waterville, Maine • London • Munich

First published in 2005 by Orpheus Books Ltd., 2 Church Green, Witney, Oxfordshire, OX28 4AW

First published in North America in 2006 by Thomson Gale

Copyright © 2006 Orpheus Books Ltd.

Created and produced: Rachel Coombs, Nicholas Harris, Sarah Harrison, Sarah Hartley, Emma Helbrough, Orpheus Books Ltd.

Text: Nicholas Harris

Consultant: David Hawksett, astronomer, writer and broadcaster

Illustrator: Sebastian Quigley (*Linden Artists*),Gary Hincks

For more information, contact
Blackbirch Press
27500 Drake Rd.
Farmington Hills, MI 48331-3535
Or you can visit our Internet site at http://www.gale.com

Permissions Department
The Gale Group, Inc.
27500 Drake Rd.
Farmington Hills, MI 48331-3535
248-699-8006 or 800-877-4253, ext. 8006
Fax: 248-699-8074 or 800-762-4058

LIBRARY OF CONGRESS CATALOGING-IN-PUBLICATIONS

Harris, Nicholas.
    Stars and planets / by Nicholas Harris.
        p. cm. -- (First library of knowledge)
    ISBN 1-4103-0343-8 (hardcover : alk. paper) 1. Stars--Juvenile literature. 2. Planets--Juvenile literature. I. Title. II. Series.

QB801.7.H365 2006
522--dc22   2005029615

Printed in Malaysia
10 9 8 7 6 5 4 3 2 1

CONTENTS

INTRODUCTION

SPACE is the vast, dark expanse beyond our own planet Earth. Distances in space are enormous. Even the nearest star is so far away that light shining from it takes more than four years to reach Earth. (Light travels at about 186,400 miles [300,000 kilometers] per second.) And some stars lie several billion times farther away!

Planet

Comet

Moon

THE NIGHT SKY

THE STARS are always shining in the sky. It is only when the nearest star, the Sun, sets at night that we can see them. Stars produce their own light. **Comets,** planets, and the Moon all reflect the light of the Sun. Shooting stars are tiny fragments of rock, called meteors, that burn up in the Earth's atmosphere.

Milky Way

Meteors

MILKY WAY

All the stars that we can see with the naked eye belong to the Milky Way galaxy. It is a vast spiral of hundreds of billions of stars. From the Earth, one of the galaxy's spiral arms looks like a misty band stretching across the sky. Our Sun is situated on one of the four spiral arms, halfway out from the center.

CONSTELLATIONS

ONSTELLATIONS are patterns of stars in the sky. People once thought they looked like gods, heroes, or animals from legends. Different constellations can be seen in the northern and southern skies.

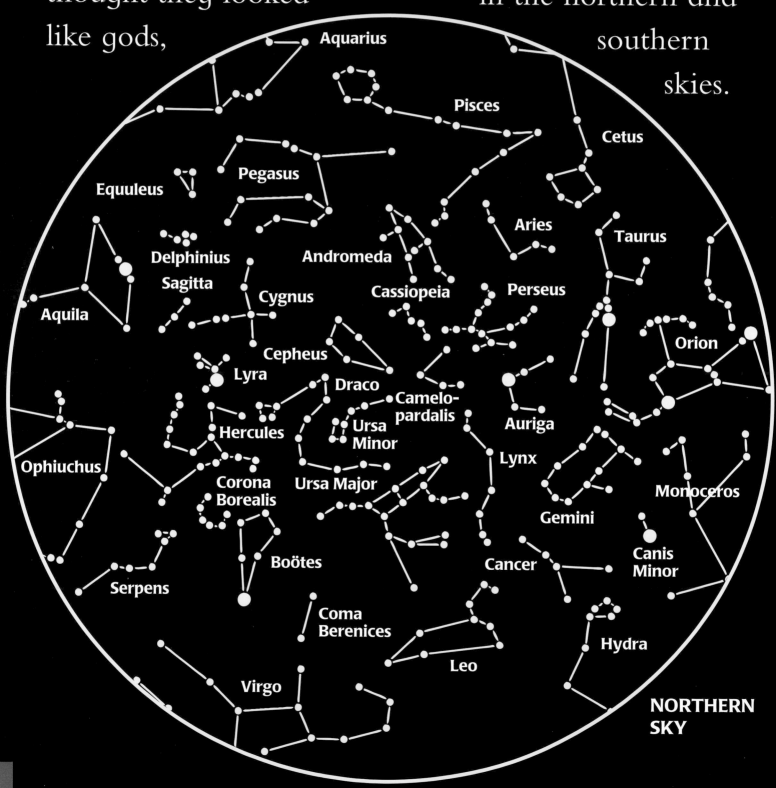

Aquarius

Pisces

Cetus

Pegasus

Equuleus

Aries

Taurus

Delphinius

Andromeda

Sagitta

Cygnus

Cassiopeia

Perseus

Aquila

Cepheus

Orion

Lyra

Draco

Camelo-pardalis

Auriga

Hercules

Ursa Minor

Ophiuchus

Lynx

Monoceros

Corona Borealis

Ursa Major

Gemini

Boötes

Cancer

Canis Minor

Serpens

Coma Berenices

Hydra

Virgo

Leo

NORTHERN SKY

ORION THE HUNTER

Orion, visible in both northern and southern skies, is an easy constellation to spot. Three stars form his **diagonal** belt, while others trace out his club and shield. The belt stars point down towards Sirius, the brightest star in the night sky.

Pisces

Cetus

Aquarius

Eridanus

Sculptor

Phoenix

Grus

Fornax

Capricornus

Tucana

Aquila

Lepus

Reticulum

Sagittarius

Columba

Dorado

Pavo

Orion

Octans

Scorpius

Canis Major

Carina

Crux

Ophiuchus

Vela

Lupus

Monoceros

Puppis

Centaurus

Pyxis

Libra

Hydra

Corvus

Crater

Virgo

Sextans

SOUTHERN SKY

SOLAR SYSTEM

THE SUN lies at the center of the solar system. This consists of the nine planets, their moons, and **asteroids**, **meteoroids**, comets (*see page 25*), and vast amounts of gas and dust. The planets orbit (move around) the Sun in a **counterclockwise** direction.

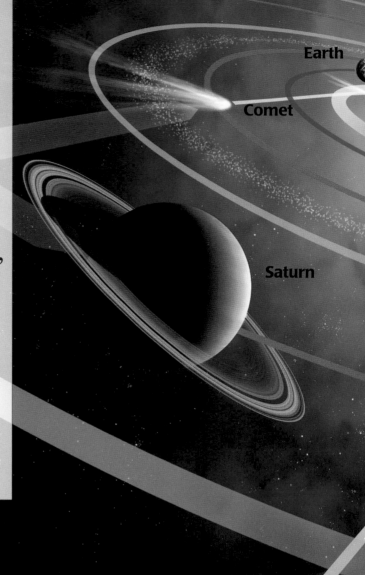

Earth

Comet

Saturn

Neptune

Sun Mercury Venus Earth Mars	Asteroids	Jupiter	Saturn	Uranus

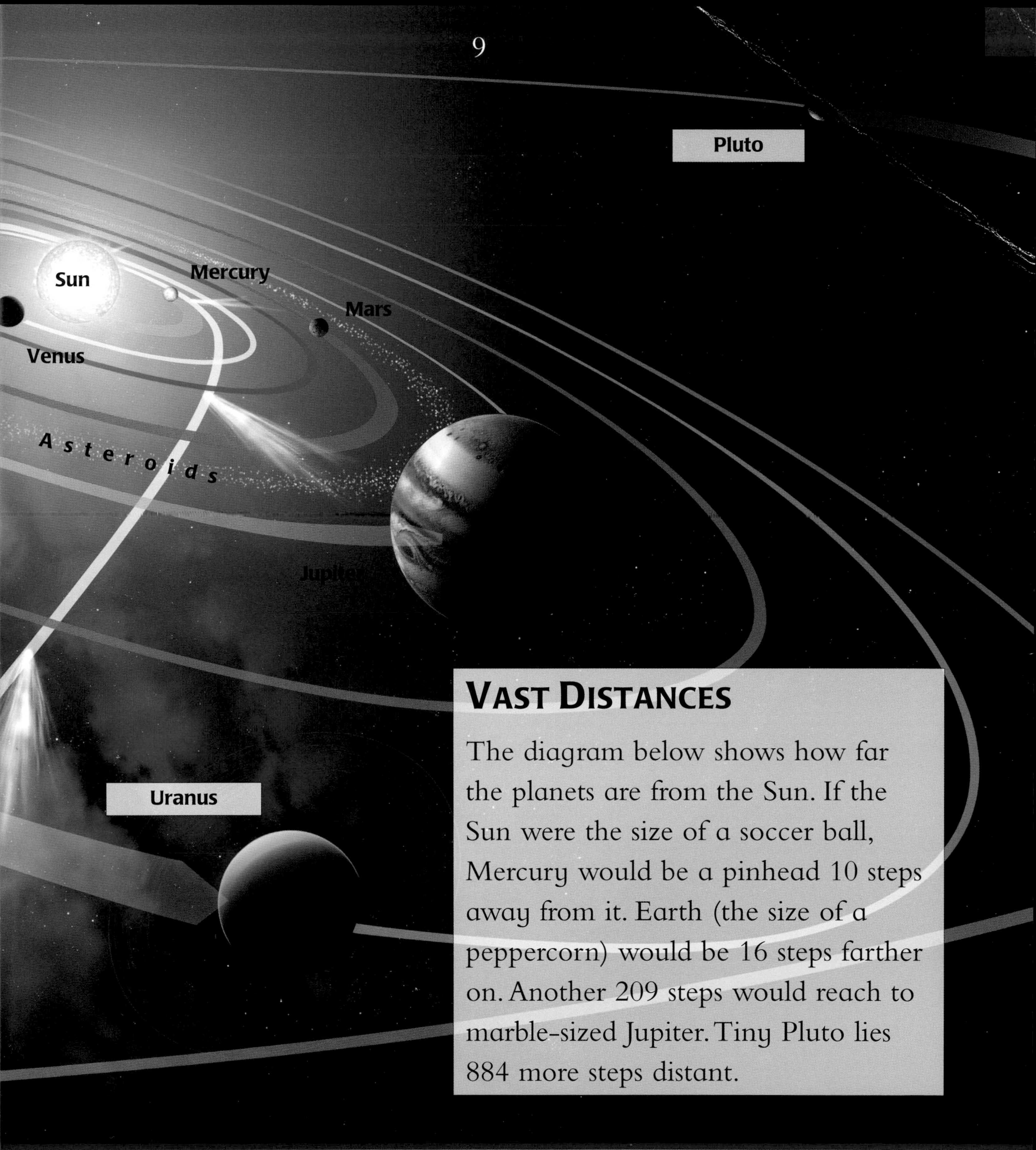

Sun

Mercury

Venus

Mars

A s t e r o i d s

Jupiter

Uranus

Pluto

VAST DISTANCES

The diagram below shows how far the planets are from the Sun. If the Sun were the size of a soccer ball, Mercury would be a pinhead 10 steps away from it. Earth (the size of a peppercorn) would be 16 steps farther on. Another 209 steps would reach to marble-sized Jupiter. Tiny Pluto lies 884 more steps distant.

Pluto
(when nearest the Sun)

Neptune

Pluto
(at its farthest point from the Sun)

THE PHASES OF THE MOON

THE MOON is our nearest neighbor in space. It is a ball of rock a quarter the size of the Earth. It orbits our planet in just over 27 days. The same face always points toward the Earth.

When the Sun lights up the whole of the near side of the Moon, we see a full moon.

5 Full moon

6 Gibbous moon

8 Crescent moon

7 Quarter moon

The sequence above shows the changing shape of the Moon as it orbits the Earth (below). The numbers show the position of the moon on its 27-day journey.

THE CHANGING MOON

The Moon seems to change shape from one night to the next. But it is really our view of the part of the Moon that is lit up by the Sun that changes. When the face pointed toward us is turned away from the Sun, we cannot see it at all. As the Moon orbits the Earth, more and more of it is lit, until it is fully turned towards the Sun. This is the full moon.

4 Gibbous moon

5 Full Moon

6 Gibbous moon

4 Gibbous moon

2 Crescent moon

1 New Moon

3 Quarter moon

SOLAR ECLIPSE

The Moon and Sun appear to be about the same size in the sky. So when the Moon passes between the Earth and Sun, it sometimes blocks out our view of the Sun completely. This is a total eclipse. The Sun's atmosphere, called the corona, shines out from behind the moon.

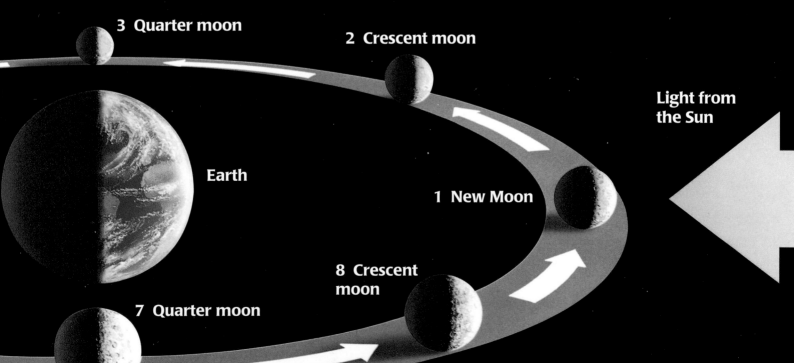

3 Quarter moon

2 Crescent moon

Light from the Sun

Earth

1 New Moon

8 Crescent moon

7 Quarter moon

THE MOON

THE MOON is a barren world. It has neither air nor liquid water, so no plants and animals can live there. There is no soil—only bare rock and dust.

Craters are found all over the Moon. Most were formed millions of years ago when meteorites *(see page 25)* crashed into the lunar surface, blasting huge basins out of the rock.

When meteorites punched out craters, debris was scattered in all directions. This left streaks in the lunar surface. With no wind to cover them over, these streaks are still there after millions of years.

Streaks

CRATERS AND "SEAS"

The Moon is covered by thousands of craters. There are also dark lava plains, formed when molten rock seeped out from under the ground. Many years ago, observers from Earth thought these dark areas might be seas. They are still called by the Latin word for sea, *mare*.

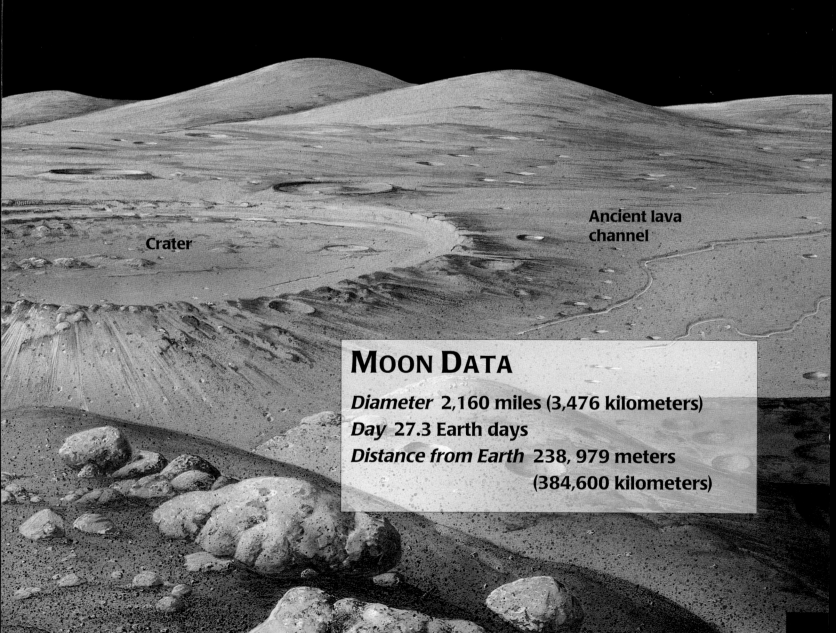

Crater

Ancient lava channel

MOON DATA

Diameter 2,160 miles (3,476 kilometers)
Day 27.3 Earth days
Distance from Earth 238, 979 meters
(384,600 kilometers)

MERCURY AND VENUS

MILLIONS of years ago, Mercury was bombarded by meteorites, boulders falling from space. They punched thousands of craters into its barren, rocky surface.

Venus is permanently covered in thick clouds. These are made not of water, but droplets of deadly sulfuric acid. The air, made of carbon dioxide, is unbreathable.

There are many thousands of volcanoes on Venus. Lava, molten rock from inside the planet, has cut channels in the ground. Smaller, dome-shaped volcanoes known as "pancakes" are formed when lava oozes to the surface and cools.

"Pancake" volcano

MERCURY DATA

Diameter 3,031 miles (4,878 kilometers)
Day 58.6 Earth days
Year 88 Earth days
Distance from the Sun 36 million miles (58 million kilometers)
Moons None

HIGH TEMPERATURES

Venus

Venus is the hottest planet in the solar system. Its dense **atmosphere**, the blanket of

Mercury

gases that surrounds it, prevents the heat from escaping. The temperature on Venus is always the same. It is high enough to melt lead. On Mercury, it is also extremely hot, but only by day. During the long nights, temperatures can drop to -274°F (-170°C).

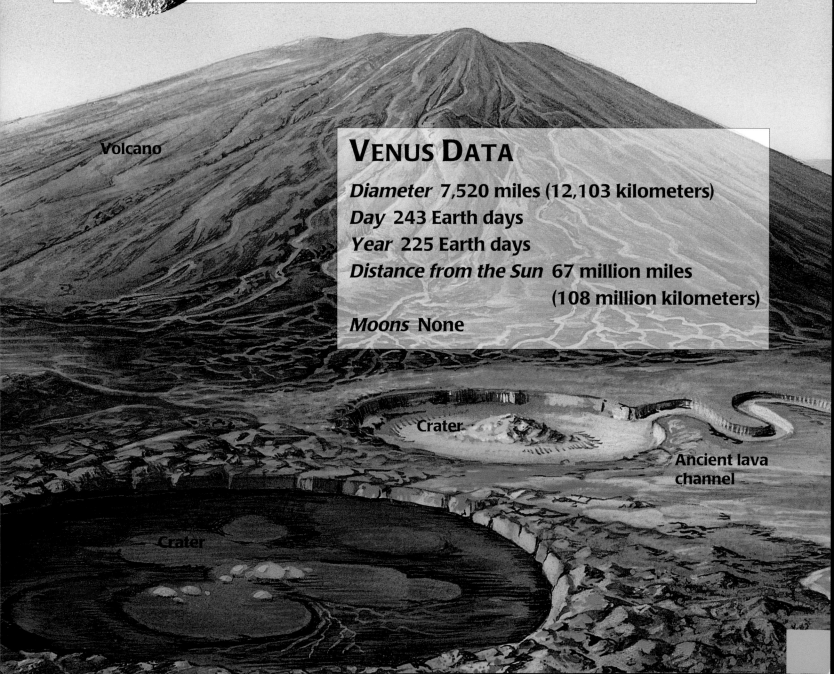

Volcano

VENUS DATA

Diameter 7,520 miles (12,103 kilometers)
Day 243 Earth days
Year 225 Earth days
Distance from the Sun 67 million miles
(108 million kilometers)
Moons None

Crater

Ancient lava channel

Crater

MARS

MARS is the planet most like Earth. It has volcanoes and valleys. There are four seasons. Although temperatures are usually cold, it can be quite warm in summer.

It is possible that there was once life on Mars. There may be still. Dry riverbeds and old seashores prove that water once flowed there. Water is vital for life.

This is a view of a Martian valley. The slopes are lined with small channels. They were probably made by running water.

Crater

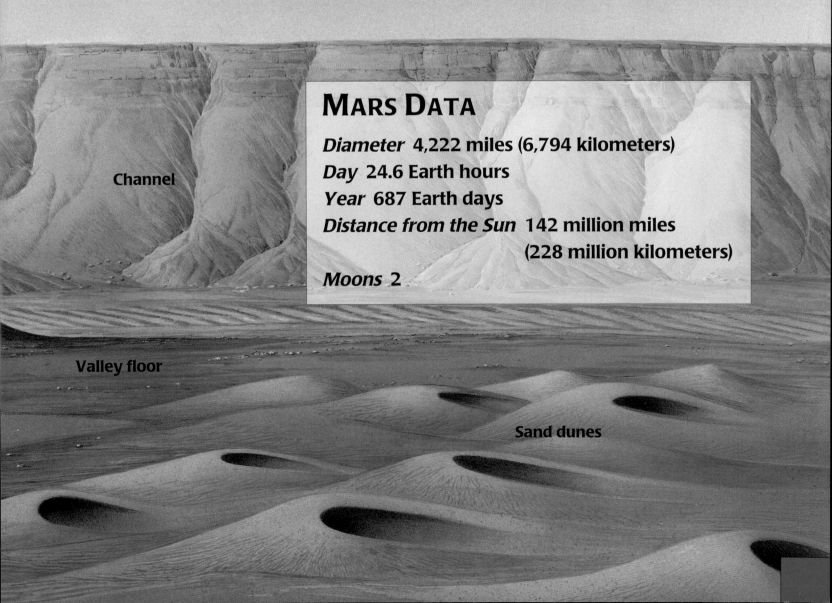

RED PLANET

Mars is known as the Red Planet because of the reddish color of the dust that covers it. Sometimes dark areas of rock show up when storms blow away the dust. Like Earth, Mars has ice caps at both its north and south poles. These are made of water and carbon dioxide ice.

Channel

MARS DATA

Diameter 4,222 miles (6,794 kilometers)
Day 24.6 Earth hours
Year 687 Earth days
Distance from the Sun 142 million miles
(228 million kilometers)
Moons 2

Valley floor

Sand dunes

JUPITER

JUPITER, the largest planet, does not have a solid surface at all. Like Saturn, Uranus, and Neptune, it is a gas giant.

The bands of red, white, brown, and yellow are thick clouds swirling around the globe. They cause constant storms.

Volcanic eruption

Jupiter as seen from Io

Pool of molten rock

THE KING OF PLANETS

Large enough to contain more than 1,300 Earths, Jupiter is bigger than all the other planets combined. The Great Red Spot is a storm that has been raging for 300 years. It is three times the size of the Earth.

JUPITER DATA

Diameter 88, 784 miles (142,884 kilometers)
Day 9.8 Earth hours
Year 11.8 Earth years
Distance from the Sun 484 million miles
(778 million kilometers)
Moons 63

Jupiter's moon Io is covered by volcanoes and pools of molten rock. The volcanoes erupt sulfur dioxide gas 186 miles (300 kilometers) skyward.

SATURN

THE SECOND largest planet, Saturn, is famous for its magnificent rings. Three broad rings can be seen through a telescope from Earth. The outer ring is separated from the inner two by a gap. The rings, actually thousands of narrow ringlets, are made up of billions of small blocks of ice and rock.

Saturn, as seen from Titan

Drainage channel

SATURN DATA

Diameter 74,898 miles (120,536 kilometers)
Day 10.2 Earth hours
Year 29.4 Earth years
Distance from the Sun 887 million miles
(1,427 million kilometers)
Moons 31

THE RINGED PLANET

Saturn's rings are 170,877 miles (275,000 kilometers) wide, rim to rim. They are between 328 feet (100 meters) and 0.6 miles (1 kilometer) thick.

Like Jupiter, Saturn is a gas giant. It spins very quickly, causing a bulge around its center. Storm clouds swirl around its globe. If a large enough tub could be found, Saturn would float on the water!

"Lake"

Titan, Saturn's largest moon, is the only moon in the solar system to have a thick atmosphere. In January 2005, the lander *Huygens* was released from the space probe *Cassini* and landed on Titan's surface. It sent back pictures showing drainage channels and what could be tar-encrusted lakes.

URANUS AND NEPTUNE

URANUS is a large ball of gas. There are almost no surface features. It is tilted on its side. That means as Uranus orbits the Sun, first one pole faces the Sun for 42 Earth years, then the other pole faces the Sun for 42 years.

Uranus

Cliff

Rings of
Uranus

URANUS DATA

Diameter 31,763 miles (51,118 kilometers)
Day 17.2 Earth hours
Year 84 Earth years
Distance from the Sun 1.78 billion miles
(2.87 billion
kilometers)
Moons 27

Canyon

Crater

BLUE PLANET

Like Uranus, Neptune is a blue ball of gas. Only a few wispy white clouds and dark spots can be seen on its surface. They are carried round the planet at 1,243 miles (2,000 kilometers) per hour. Both Uranus and Neptune have faint, dark rings.

NEPTUNE DATA

Diameter 31,403 miles (50,538 kilometers)
Day 16.1 Earth hours
Year 164.8 Earth years
Distance from the Sun 2.79 million miles (4.5 million kilometers)

Moons 13

The surface of Uranus's moon Miranda has deep canyons, high cliffs, long grooves, and wide craters.

PLUTO, COMETS, AND ASTEROIDS

PLUTO was not discovered until 1930. It is the smallest, coldest, and outermost planet of the solar system. From its surface, the Sun would look no bigger than a bright star. Pluto's permanently frozen landscape is probably pitted with craters. Its moon, Charon, is just over half its size.

Charon

PLUTO DATA

Diameter 1,444 miles (2,324 kilometers)
Day 6.4 Earth days
Year 248 Earth years
Distance from the Sun
  3.67 billion miles (5.9
  billion kilometers)
Moons 1

Nucleus of comet

DIRTY SNOWBALLS

Comets are lumps of dust and ice. Like the planets, comets orbit the Sun. When they near it, the ice melts. Long tails of gas and dust stretch out— always pointing away from the Sun.

Gas tail (straight)

Dust tail (curved)

Asteroid

ASTEROIDS

Thousands of small potato-shaped lumps of rock or metal orbit the Sun between Mars and Jupiter. Called asteroids, they are probably the remains of a planet that was smashed apart billions of years ago. Fragments of asteroids, called meteoroids, travel around the solar system. When they crash to Earth, they are known as meteorites.

THE SUN

ALTHOUGH fairly small when compared to many other stars, the Sun, our nearest star, is enormous compared to the planets. It produces huge amounts of energy at its core. This shines out across the solar system. The Sun's light and heat are vital for life on Earth.

Arch

Sometimes huge arches of glowing gas appear. They are held up by magnetism, an invisible force.

SUN DATA

Diameter 863,706 miles
(1,390,000 kilometers)
Length of time it takes to spin (at its equator)
25.4 Earth days
Surface temperature
9,932°F (5,500°C)

Jupiter
(to scale)

Earth
(to scale)

Prominence

Flares are sudden big explosions of energy. They can reach millions of miles into space.

The surface of the Sun bubbles and spits like water boiling in a pan.

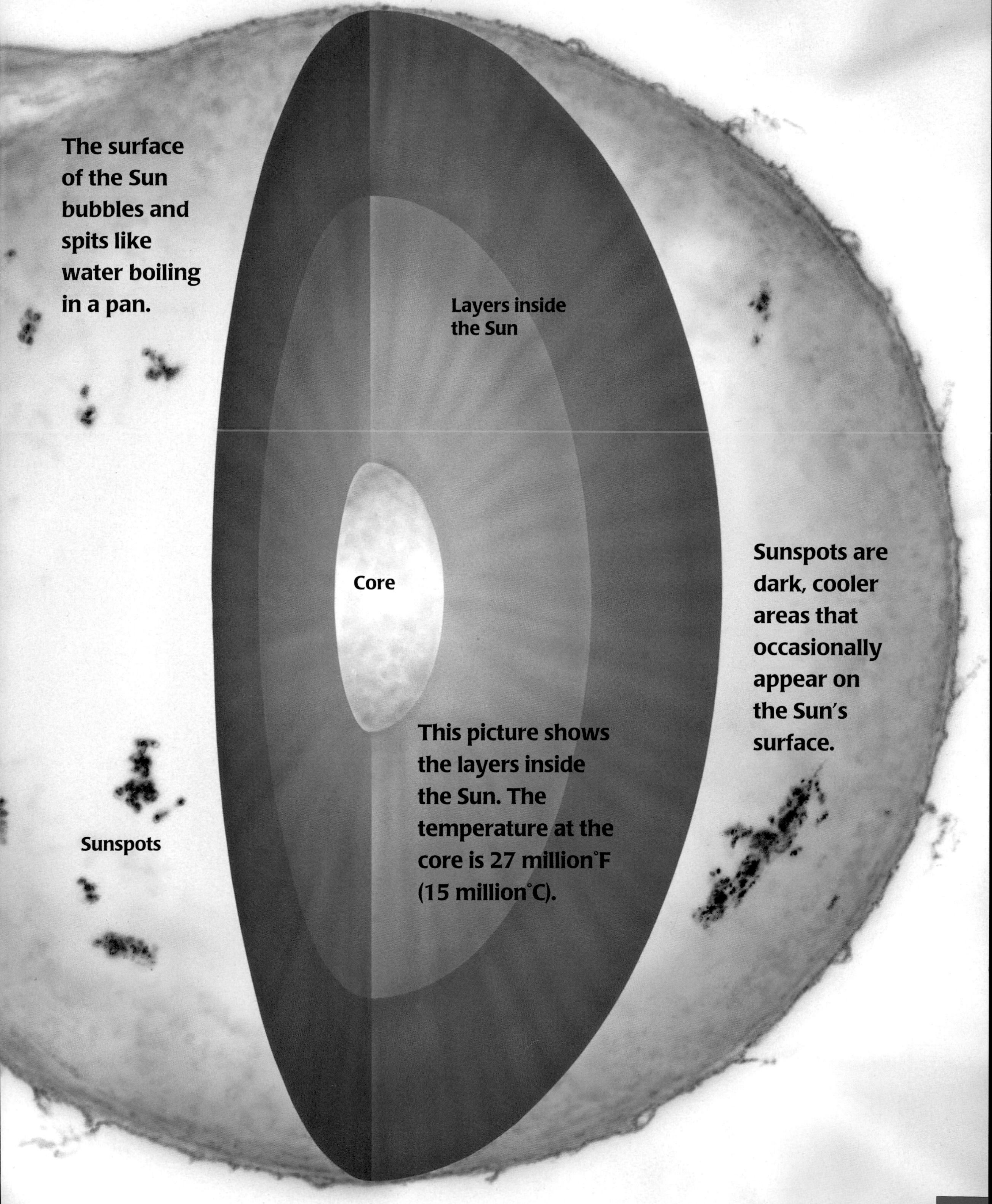

Layers inside the Sun

Core

Sunspots

This picture shows the layers inside the Sun. The temperature at the core is 27 million°F (15 million°C).

Sunspots are dark, cooler areas that occasionally appear on the Sun's surface.

Stars

STARS are giant, hot spinning balls of gas. They give off massive amounts of energy, including light and heat.

All over space are colorful clouds of dust and gas, called nebulae. Eventually stars will form from these clouds.

GIANTS AND DWARFS

Stars come in many colors and sizes. The largest star in this scale illustration is the red supergiant Betelgeuse. Next are the blue giants Rigel and Polaris (the Pole Star). The Sun (a yellow dwarf) is the small yellow dot.

THE UNIVERSE

THE UNIVERSE is everything we know. All matter, from the tiniest worm to the most gigantic star, is part of the universe. It even includes empty space.

The universe probably began in an incredible explosion, called the Big Bang. It happened about 13.7 billion years ago.

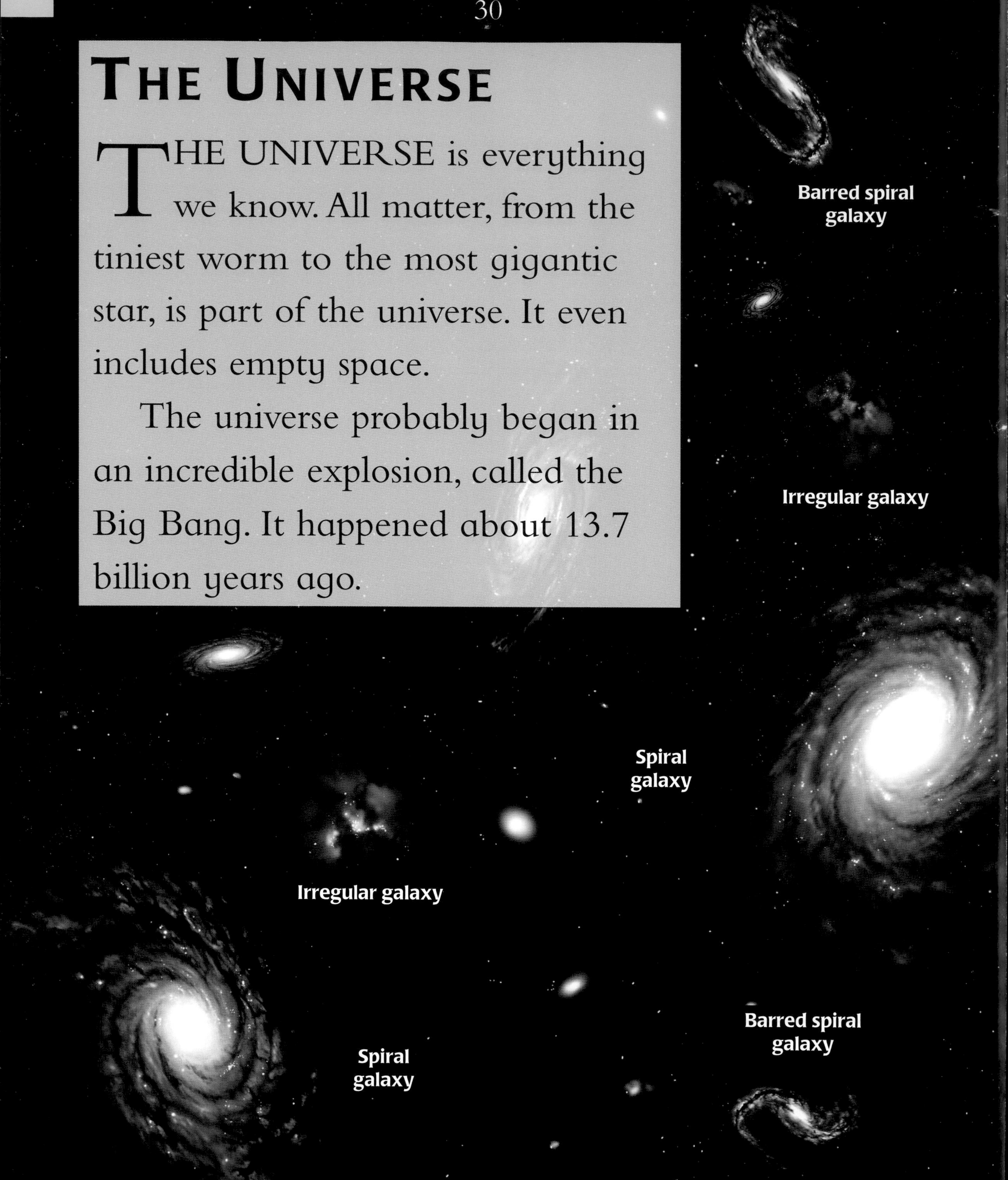

Barred spiral galaxy

Irregular galaxy

Spiral galaxy

Irregular galaxy

Spiral galaxy

Barred spiral galaxy

Spiral galaxy

Elliptical galaxy

Elliptical galaxy

Barred spiral galaxy

GALAXIES OF STARS

The universe is made up of billions of galaxies—swirling masses of hundreds of billions of stars. These galaxies are not spread out evenly, but grouped in clusters. Our own solar system belongs to the Milky Way galaxy (see page 5). It is part of a cluster of about 30 galaxies called the Local Group. The galaxies in this cluster are of several different types: spirals (like the Milky Way), barred spirals, ellipticals (shaped like ovals), and irregulars (no obvious shape).

GLOSSARY

asteroid: Lumps of rock or metal that orbit the Sun.

atmosphere: A mixture of gases that surrounds the Earth and many other planets.

comet: Lumps of dust and ice that orbit the Sun.

counterclockwise: The direction opposite the movement of the hands of a clock.

diagonal: Slanted at an angle.

meteoroids: Fragments of asteroids that travel through the solar system.

nucleus: Center.

INDEX